Michael Kitson

REMBRANDT

PHAIDON

Phaidon Press Limited, Littlegate House, St Ebbe's Street, Oxford
Published in the United States of America by E. P. Dutton, New York

First published 1969
Third edition, revised, 1978

ISBN 0 7148 1876 3
Library of Congress Catalog Card Number: 77-92107

Printed in Great Britain by Waterlow (Dunstable) Limited

REMBRANDT

When we stand in the Rembrandt room of a major picture gallery, what visual impressions do we receive and how do they differ from the impressions we receive from other rooms in the same gallery?

To begin with, we notice dark backgrounds broken by irregular patches of light. There is more dark than light, and the light is not often taken up to the frame. Instead, it lies towards the centre where it balances the dark and acts as the focus of greatest interest. Usually there are both black and white in the picture, the black occurring in a robe or hat, the white in a collar, cuffs or else in a headcloth or shirtfront. The frames are also sometimes black. Black and white represent colours – the only unmodified colours in the picture – but they also register as extremes of light and dark tones.

Otherwise the paintings are rich in colour but it is not pure or evenly applied colour; nor is the composition divided into fields of different colours as in Renaissance or modern painting. Even in Rembrandt's early works the colours are broken and changing, like a brocade woven with gold or silver threads or like the glowing embers of a fire. In the highlights and deepest shadows the colours almost disappear. In the middle tones they deepen and become more intense in one of two directions: either towards red (vermilion or madder lake) or towards greenish-gold. It is typical that Rembrandt uses these colours as alternatives, not together, so that red and green seldom appear in combination. He generally avoids colour contrasts and complementaries and prefers colours close to each other in the spectrum. Brown, orange or yellow are mixed with or appear beside red; yellow or dull green accompany and merge into greenish-gold. Grey is also used with his two main colours. Blues, violets, pinks and bright greens, however, occur only in pale tints and in subordinate positions. The early paintings are generally cool in colour, the mature and late ones warm, with red predominating. Like the strongest lights, the strongest colours are confined to only a comparatively small part of the picture. The effect is of a surge of colour coming from within the form rather than of colour decorating the surface, defining the form's shape.

The backgrounds are also of no single colour but are made up of dull browns, greens and greys, usually blended together but in the late works sometimes laid on side by side. Unlike the backgrounds of some Italian baroque painters, Rembrandt's are never flat or opaque but are filled with atmosphere and penetrated by reflected light. (Only uncleaned paintings by Rembrandt give an impression of solid dark brown in the shadows.) These more subdued neutral colours register as tones. Tone, or rather *chiaroscuro*, is the basis of Rembrandt's art. Colour, however important and beautiful, is contingent. It may be quite strong or very restrained; some paintings are almost monochromatic, and a few are executed in *grisaille*. But whatever its strength, colour is an adjunct. The scheme of the composition is established by the *chiaroscuro*. Colour is applied in some parts, where it attracts the eye and heightens the emotional tension, but not in others. Only in certain late works does colour become a semi-independent medium, and even occasionally predominate (Pl. 43). Elsewhere it is integrated with the *chiaroscuro*. *Chiaroscuro* is the principal means both of 'keeping together the overall harmony' (as Rembrandt's earliest biographer, Sandrart, put it) and of creating a poetic mood; it is also a source of aesthetic pleasure and of luminous and striking effects in its own right. Rembrandt's mastery of *chiaroscuro*, in all its degrees from the darkest darks to the strongest lights, has been acknowledged ever since his own time.

In composition, Rembrandt's paintings are essentially simple and stable and are built up from the edges towards the centre. Secondary lights, colours and forms are subordinated to primary ones. Rembrandt does not divide up the design into self-contained units or distribute the interest among different areas. Visually the design obeys a principle of hierarchy. Except in his earliest works there is no sense of overcrowding or strain. Movement continues to be represented later (during his 'baroque' period) but after a while it too largely disappears. At all stages of his development his figures possess great authority and presence. They are set against a background which is vague and neutral enough not to compete with them yet which is everywhere visually interesting. Thus the background forms part of the design, it is not a mere backcloth. It also serves to relax the tension which exists at and near the centre and to effect a smooth transition from the imagined world of the main action or figure to the real world of the spectator.

Elegance, *contrapposto*, the harmony and balance of parts – those foundations on which the beautiful rests in Renaissance painting – are conspicuous by their absence. Except in Rembrandt's most baroque paintings there are no swinging lines and few three-dimensional curves or forms leading the eye into depth. He sometimes borrows from, but is never dependent upon, conventional formulas of the ideal and the beautiful. He uses flat, often rather fastidious and simple shapes lying parallel to the picture surface, especially in his late period, but not graceful, sweeping contours or variations of the S-curve common to mannerist, baroque and rococo painters. When he does introduce a curving or flowing line he interrupts its rhythm with some irregular twist or sudden change in pace. Generally speaking, flowing lines are weak in Rembrandt; energetic lines are jagged or straight. In some of his late works he builds up a pattern of rectangles and triangles, and occasionally a large circle or disc appears in the background. After the early years of his career, in keeping with his unwillingness to use a stressed contour, he tends to avoid figures and faces in profile. He prefers to contain the most interesting visual effects within the contour of the form, as in the 'Jewish Bride' (Pl. 39), in which the husband's right hand and both the wife's form a pattern of hands in the centre of the composition.

To an unusual degree Rembrandt's art – not only in his portraits but also in his subject pictures – is dominated by faces; few of them are handsome and many of the most remarkable are old. Their watchful eyes are indistinct and often in shadow except for a line of light along the lids. His faces are always expressive and habitually tense. An urge to communicate thought, feeling and experience is imprinted on them. Although partly shadowed, they are seen in close-up, as if the artist were peering at them and they were returning his gaze. From the works of few other artists do we get such a sense of watching and of being watched. It is not an accident that about two-thirds of Rembrandt's paintings are portraits (including some fifty of himself). Most of the rest in our hypothetical Rembrandt room will be scenes or figures from the Bible. In addition, there will probably be a mythological scene, a landscape and perhaps a *genre* scene or still life. The paintings are likely to vary greatly in size and to range from the very small to the quite large.

Permeating all Rembrandt's works of whatever category and size is an air of solemnity and mystery. He is not a frivolous or merely sensuous artist, nor does he delight in beauty of colour or brushwork for their own sake. When colour and brushwork are beautiful, as they often are, they are so for expressive rather than decorative reasons. Moreover, the solemn and the mysterious are attributes of Rembrandt's style, not merely of his attitude to the subject matter. To veil forms, textures and colours, leaving something for the imagination to fill in, is central to his method. A tone, a background, suggests more than it states; the eye can only trace out its implications so far. The world of Rembrandt's paintings is certainly as imaginary as that of any painter working in an ideal style: he does not take us into the open air or reconstruct a real interior. Yet, unlike the world of most such painters, his is not raised above nature; it appears to us rather as an intensified vision of nature's essential reality. Rembrandt reverses the normal procedure of idealizing artists. Whereas they transform the essence of things and leave a reminder of nature in the details, he preserves reality in the essence and clothes its outward forms with a mysterious beauty and suggestiveness.

It is useful to begin thus by recalling some of the aesthetic characteristics of Rembrandt's paintings, because for over a hundred years the praise of Rembrandt has often been less aesthetic than moral. His work has been treated as the product not so much of a visual artist as of a superior, almost God-like personality. The emphasis has fallen on his possession of qualities of character: dedication, humanity, compassion, spiritual and psychological insight, courage to ignore fashion and to refuse to flatter patrons, above all, unswerving devotion to 'the truth' – the truth about himself, his sitters and the events and characters of the Bible. These qualities are immediately attractive nowadays. We admire integrity and independence of spirit in artists. Nor is it intrinsically an error to see Rembrandt in this light, although it is possible to exaggerate the extent to which he possessed some of the virtues attributed to him. Nevertheless, it is important to be aware of what has happened, so to speak. That is to say, we should realize that much of the modern tendency of Rembrandt appreciation is due to developments in art criticism since his time and that what we see in his work may not have been present, either to the minds and eyes of his contemporaries, or in the consciousness of Rembrandt himself. For some reason this problem is particularly acute where Rembrandt is concerned. It may be so partly because contemporary information about his *art* is very hard to obtain, whereas his personality – and hence by unconscious inference his mind – is deceptively accessible, through documents relating to his life, through his self-portraits, through his portraits of his family, and so on. But whatever the reason, the result has been to divert attention from Rembrandt the artist to Rembrandt the man. Thus there has emerged a sentimental cult of Rembrandt, which is not by any means confined to popular or old-fashioned literature; this cult presents us with Rembrandt the home-lover, the paragon of virtue and the sage.

It is not easy to tell how far the modern Rembrandt, even without the sentimental distortions, is the invention, and how far the discovery, of later critics. It would be as foolish to ignore the insights of the past hundred and fifty years as it would be to accept them without question. What is certain is that they were made possible by a radical shift in the methods of criticism which began in the Romantic period. The practice of previous critics had been to assess the qualities of a work of art by examining the work itself; the tendency now was to look beyond the work and to seek for the key to its qualities in the artist's mind. The significance of this development for the understanding of Rembrandt is so great that it is worth discussing it a little further.

Until the Romantics, works of art had been judged by more or less objective standards: whether they were beautiful or ugly, true or false to nature, and whether or not they were treated in accordance with certain rules. They were examined piecemeal, under the headings of drawing, colour, composition, etc. With the coming of Romanticism, standards became at once more comprehensive and more subjective. Sincerity was used as a criterion of artistic judgement for the first time and new kinds of truth were brought into the argument. Was the artist true to his own inner vision and experience (that is, was he sincere)? Did he, as Goethe expressed it, 'love what he painted and paint only what he loved'? Was he true not just to the letter but to the spirit of his subject matter? In this way the critical interest was shifted from the work of art to the artist's total attitude.

As a result of these developments, what had previously been regarded as faults or at best limitations in Rembrandt came to be considered merits. His 'low' subjects and interest in and association with the poor, the old and the Jews, which had been condemned as undignified, now marked him out as the champion of the downtrodden and the oppressed; hence the concept of Rembrandt's compassion emerged. His broad brushwork and disregard of the rules of proportion and anatomy, which had been thought ignorant and eccentric, were now interpreted as a refusal to sacrifice his convictions for the sake of easy fame; hence arose the idea of Rembrandt's integrity. His common, naturalistic style, once thought fit only for comic and vulgar subjects, was now felt to be better suited to scenes from the Bible than the ideal style of the Italians, since those scenes took place in humble surroundings and were enacted by humble people; hence came the discovery of Rembrandt's spiritual insight and regard for truth.

The question of the special appropriateness of Rembrandt's style for religious subject matter is of particular interest, as it has played so large a part in modern criticism and in forming the popular image of Rembrandt today. Probably the first to discuss this point was Goethe, in the essay from which the phrase quoted earlier was taken (*Nach Falkonet und über Falkonet*, 1776). This essay already contains, in essence, everything that has been said on the subject since, and says it with a moderation not always found in later writings. Rembrandt is seen as having created a new form of religious art, as valid in its way as Raphael's was in another way. Indeed, his style had the advantage over Italian Renaissance painting in being truer than the latter to the spirit of the Bible, and hence of being fresher and more capable of communicating the Christian message with an appropriate directness and force.

'When Rembrandt represents his Madonna and Child as a Dutch peasant woman, it is easy for every refined gentleman to see that this is historically inaccurate, since we are told that Christ was born in Bethlehem of Judea. The Italians were better at this! he says. And how, please? – did Raphael paint anything other, anything more, than a loving mother with her first-born and only son? and what else could have been made of the subject? Has not mother-love in its joys and sorrows been a fruitful subject for poets and painters in all ages? But all the Bible stories have been deprived of their simplicity and truth by cold grandeur and stiff ecclesiastical propriety, and have thus been withdrawn from sympathetic hearts in order to dazzle the gaping eyes of the stupid. Does not Mary sit between the scrolls of every altar-frame, before the shepherds, as if she were displaying her Child for money, or as if she had rested for four weeks after her confinement so as to prepare with the vanity of a lady for the honour of this visit? Now that's decent! that's proper! that doesn't trespass against history!

How does Rembrandt treat this subject [the etching of *The Adoration of the Shepherds*, about 1656–7]? He places us in a dark stable; necessity has driven the mother, the Child at her breast, to share a bed with the cattle. They are both wrapped to the neck in straw and rags, and everything is dark outside the glow from a small lamp which shines on the father, who sits there with a small book and appears to read Mary a prayer. At this moment the shepherds enter. The foremost of them, who advances with a stable-lantern, peers, taking off his cap, into the straw. Was it possible more clearly to express the question: Is this the new-born King of the Jews?'

The key to this passage lies in the change of tone at the beginning of the second paragraph. No-one before had described a composition by Rembrandt so literally and so sympathetically or had so well caught its spirit of simple humility. Here for the first time Rembrandt is presented as the painter of and for the human heart.

As has already been said, these considerations are not irrelevant or invalid. There is no doubt that Rembrandt did introduce a new kind of religious art, based on a literal rather than symbolic interpretation of the Bible. What is more, whoever looks at his work, and not only at his religious paintings but also at his portraits and even landscapes, cannot help seeing it as a moral as well as aesthetic achievement. But while this is true, it is a method of approach to Rembrandt which lies in the background of this essay, whose purpose is, rather, to return to an older tradition of criticism and to discuss his paintings as works of art. Its theme is Rembrandt the artist. We see a painting of *The Holy Family with Angels* (Pl. 23). It strikes us as simultaneously domestic and sacred, lively and serene, intimate and deeply moving. How were the tones, colours and brushmarks disposed to produce these results? This is the type of question that will chiefly concern us.

Rembrandt as an Artist

Although little information relating to Rembrandt's art (as distinct from his life) has come down to us, such as it is it is not negligible and is worth briefly recalling. It appears chiefly in the following sources: the three earliest biographies of Rembrandt, by Sandrart (1675), Baldinucci (1686) and Houbraken (1718); a treatise on painting by one of his pupils, Samuel van Hoogstraten (1678); the journal of Constantyn Huygens (who visited Rembrandt and his colleague Lievens in Leyden in or about 1629); a small group of letters to Huygens from Rembrandt; the inventory of his collection of works of art (both by himself and by and after other artists), weapons and curios, drawn up at his bankruptcy in 1656; and, last but not least, his own work. By this is meant, not his work in its entirety, but those aspects of it, particularly drawings and etchings, which reveal through their subject matter the personal background to his activity as a painter. This is not the place to examine these sources in detail, as the information contained in them is often indirect and would require lengthy interpretation, but some general points emerge which are worth discussing in relation to Rembrandt's practice as an artist.

Not unnaturally, the three early biographers of Rembrandt judged him by the standards of their own time. They were by no means insensitive to his qualities and they found him to be an artist of extraordinary power. They praised his colour and *chiaroscuro* and Houbraken particularly stressed the variety and vividness of the poses of his figures and their facial expressions and gestures. On the other hand, they criticized him for being weak in drawing and for neglecting the classical rules of proportion and anatomy, especially in his treatment of the nude. His paintings were believed to be unfinished owing to their broad brushwork and heavy impasto, and he was scarcely mentioned as a painter of religious subjects; rather, he was regarded (at least by Sandrart) as a *genre* painter who mostly chose subjects to please himself from the everyday life around him.

In regarding Rembrandt in this way the biographers were applying the standards of ideal art. Nowadays it is generally agreed that where Rembrandt is concerned these standards are largely irrelevant. However, this does not mean that his attitude to them was one of simple rejection, still less that he was unaware of them. Even though he never visited Italy he had ample opportunity to study Italian paintings, drawings and engravings in collections and at auction sales in Amsterdam (as he told Huygens); he could follow the example of those of his predecessors, including his teacher Lastman, who had been to Italy; and he could read, in Dutch, Van Mander's 'Didactic Poem' on painting, published in Haarlem in 1604 as a preface to his *Lives of the Artists*, in which the theory of ideal art was fully explained. Up to a point, in fact, this theory must have furnished the aesthetic assumptions on which his own art was based – if only because there was no other articulated body of theory available. Two of its principles in particular apply: the doctrine of the superiority of history painting over all other *genres*, and the importance of illustrating a subject and depicting the emotions appropriate to it by means of gestures and facial expressions. As to the first, it should be remembered that, despite the biographers, Rembrandt was a 'history painter' hardly less than Raphael or Rubens, although of a very different kind. His works, like theirs, were scenes from sacred history and (less often) classical history and mythology – imaginative in conception, moral in content and serious in mood. So anxious was he from the first to succeed in this branch of art that he never painted a commissioned portrait in his Leyden years. It is further evident that, although there was no demand in Holland for paintings to decorate churches, Rembrandt's religious pictures, not to mention his etchings, often found buyers among private collectors.

Rembrandt's interest in the illustration of the subject and the rendering of emotion is even more significant. Overtly and dramatically in his early period, more subtly in his middle and later years, Rembrandt was one of the great story tellers of art. This did not mean only that he chose a promising situation or narrative and depicted it clearly, but also that he extracted the utmost emotional significance from it. His earliest self-portraits (see Pl. 1) are exercises in expression, and in his subject pictures throughout his career he showed feelings – in faces and in the way people stood or sat and used their hands – with a vividness and variety unsurpassed in painting. Rembrandt's skill in this art was noticed early in his career by Huygens as well as some time after his death by Houbraken. It was also the subject of the one revealing comment on art in Rembrandt's own letters, which are otherwise predominantly about money. Describing to Huygens (12 January 1639) the *Entombment* and the *Resurrection of Christ*, which he had just completed for Prince Frederick-Henry, Rembrandt states that in them he had

represented 'the greatest and most natural movement' (*die meeste ende die naetureelste beweechgelickheyt*). There is some doubt whether the last word in this phrase should be translated as movement or emotion; in fact it probably implies both (there is a similar double meaning in the English word 'moving') since mobility of poses, faces and gestures was the normal means by which emotion was expressed. In this way the phrase would be applicable not only to the *Resurrection*, in which there is a great deal of violent physical movement, but also to the outwardly calmer, though equally emotional, *Entombment*. It is an interesting coincidence that, in the same year, Poussin was writing in the same sense (but at much greater length) to his patron, Chantelou, about the depiction of emotions in *The Gathering of Manna*.

However, Rembrandt's awareness of the theory of ideal art and his acceptance of two of its most widely known principles did not mean that he was deeply interested in this theory or that he adhered to it uncritically. Although he probably had a number of aesthetic maxims which he was fond of repeating to his pupils (who in turn passed them on in garbled form to the authors of the early sources), it is unlikely that he had any fully-fledged artistic theory. And in some important respects he positively rejected the principles of ideal art. According to both Sandrart and Hoogstraten, he laid particular stress on the imitation of nature, even going so far as to state that 'the artist should be guided by nature and by no other rules'. This, if true, would have been a direct contradiction of classical principles, according to which artists should use the rules and the example of the art of the past as a means of 'correcting' nature. Furthermore, Rembrandt was not concerned with the doctrine of decorum, or the matching of style with subject matter. Nor was he committed to following the Antique, or Raphael, or the classical ideal of beauty, although he made use of all three on occasions and although his collection contained many examples of classical sculpture, either in the original or in casts, and several complete sets of engravings after Raphael. Whenever he referred to these sources in his work or painted a nude or a figure in some classical attitude, he produced a free adaptation. Even if only slightly, he undermined the system of ideal art at the point where it was most vulnerable: in its rule of internal consistency. He would interrupt the flow of a form with a quirk of realism, thicken (say) the proportions of the legs in relation to the rest of the body, or make the weight of the figure greater than its form would lead one to expect. And he did all this, unlike his Flemish and Dutch predecessors who had only half understood the classical rules, without sacrificing the organic unity of the figure or of the painting as a whole.

In his early period one can see Rembrandt almost 'attacking' the Antique. He represents the youthful Ganymede abducted by the eagle as a yelling, urinating baby. Two or three years earlier he produced a black chalk drawing of a Rubensian *Diana*, in which he made the arms and legs thinner, the flesh flabbier and the face more innocent than Rubens would have done. He subsequently used this drawing as the basis of an etching, removing the bow and quiver of Diana, adding still more creases to the flesh and turning the result into a study of an embarrassingly realistic naked woman. The object of these exercises was surely to strike a blow against art on behalf of nature, and hence on behalf of artistic freedom. But Rembrandt's destruction of the classical rules of art was also a means of understanding them. Out of this understanding grew the *Danaë* in Leningrad (1636), Rembrandt's nearest approach to a traditional classical nude. But by the standards of Titian even this is imperfect; the head and hands are too large, the facial expression is too eager and one breast is pressed out of shape by its position against the left hand. After these early experiments Rembrandt's confrontation with classicism is never so direct or thoroughgoing, either in acceptance or rejection. In his later work it is subtle, unexpected and oblique.

Freedom is the keynote of Rembrandt's relationship not only to the classical ideal, but also to other styles and traditions of art. One could make similar comparisons between his art and that of Dürer, Leonardo or Titian (who is perhaps the artist with whom his affinity is closest, although the mutual resemblance in their late work may be a coincidence). Drawing nearer Rembrandt's own country and time, there are parallels to be found with Elsheimer, Rubens and Seghers. Rembrandt's use of all these – and other – sources was selective and flexible. We have seen one example of the way in which his flexibility showed itself: in his treatment of ideal art. But the implications of his method go much further than this. He could paint 'high' subject matter in a 'low' style (breaking the rule of decorum). He could combine the beautiful and the ugly, the majestic and the intimate, the supernatural and the real. While accepting the traditional obligation to illustrate a story and represent emotions in his figures, he succeeded in evolving a new, naturalistic method of doing this. It was a method quite different from that originally devised by Italian Renaissance artists, which elsewhere in Europe during his lifetime was hardening into a formula. As will be seen later, Rembrandt's method was in effect no method, but an apparently spontaneous depiction of feelings which depended as much on the context and the *chiaroscuro* and brushwork as on the movements of the facial muscles or gestures.

Furthermore, with Rembrandt the compartments in which the different categories of painting had traditionally been kept tend to break down. Religious subjects may be treated like *genre* scenes (see Pl. 2); portraits may merge in one direction into paintings of saints or mythological characters (Pl. 11), in another direction into studies of anonymous models (Pl. 37). There is only one distinction which Rembrandt maintains: that between subjects appropriate, respectively, to drawings and to paintings (his etchings typically lie in between, overlapping each of the other two groups). Whereas his drawings include many *genre* scenes, *genre* figures and naturalistic landscapes studied from the life, his paintings on the whole do not. As a painter, Rembrandt was concerned with man as a human and spiritual being, and to have shown man in his paintings in the passing context of his day-to-day environment and activities, as he did in his drawings, would have detracted from this concern. Thus, after a few early experiments he abandoned the painting of *genre* scenes, and transferred the element of *genre* into the representation of domestic scenes from the Old and New Testament. Nor was this merely a nominal transposition, for the whole character of the subject is subtly altered, not just its outward details. In these paintings, a common Dutch pictorial form – the *genre* scene – and a deeply rooted social preoccupation – the home – are given a heightened poetic significance by their treatment as a religious subject.

It would be possible to see this characteristic in Rembrandt as a kind of idealism, and hence as the expression of an attitude similar to that which underlay the theory of ideal art. Nor would this be wrong, provided we interpret his expression of that attitude as, typically, a very personal one and regard his preoccupation with man's spiritual state more as a spontaneous development in him than as the product of any obvious outside influence. Moreover, it is reflected not only in his assimilation of *genre* subject matter to religious art, but also in his treatment of the painted single figure which was neither a portrait nor a character from the Bible or classical mythology. It is customary in catalogues and convenient for purposes of discussion to classify these figures as '*genre* studies'. But this is precisely what they are not, for they lack that distinguishing feature of *genre*, namely the element of anecdote and the hint, however slight, of activity. Rembrandt's single figures do nothing but think. To call such figures as the *Young Girl Leaning on a Window Sill* (Pl. 25) or the *Two Negroes* (Pl. 46) *genre* studies is to diminish their significance.

There is also something else. Just as these paintings have a more profound *content* than other Dutch paintings of single figures, so they have a less explicit *subject*. It is impossible to attach an allegorical label to them, like one of the Five Senses or *Vanitas*, any more than they can be called figures drinking, playing music, reading a letter or trying on a pearl necklace, for they do none of these things. Their lack of subject in the ordinary meaning of the term may be reflected in Sandrart's report that Rembrandt painted subjects 'that are ordinary and without special significance, subjects that pleased him and were picturesque (*schilderachtig*), as the people of the Netherlands say.' As a critical comment this is misleading, as it implies that Rembrandt was motivated by that idle curiosity which produces *genre*, yet the absence of an identifiable subject in these paintings was sufficiently remarkable for Sandrart to think it worth recording. It may even be the case that some of Rembrandt's paintings in which the figure is dressed in an exotic costume may belong to this category. These figures are usually interpreted nowadays as characters from the Bible – preferably obscure ones to account for the difficulty of identifying them convincingly. But Rembrandt may not have intended anything so specific, at least when he conceived the figure, although he may have attached a name to it afterwards. Perhaps even the famous and mysterious '*Polish Rider*' (Pl. 32), over which modern scholars have speculated endlessly in the attempt to find a title that would fit, is a painting of this type. Be that as it may, Rembrandt's development of the single-figure study with no explicit subject as a serious independent art form was not the least of his contributions to the future of European painting.

The Subject Pictures

The term 'subject pictures' here covers paintings, whether of religious or mythological themes, in which a situation or story is represented. In this section we shall be concerned with the way Rembrandt developed his style and technique in these pictures, which for obvious reasons usually contain two or more figures. The problems of the single figure, which have already been touched on, will be discussed further in the next section, under portraits.

Rembrandt's earliest subject pictures (Pls. 2, 3) are small, crowded and highly finished. They are designed to be examined minutely at close range. In style and often in subject they depend on his teacher, Lastman; they also contain echoes, transmitted through Lastman, of the intense, exotic art of Elsheimer. Their subjects tend to be taken from some minor episode in the Bible or from ancient history, which lent itself to the narrative treatment familiar to contemporary Dutch artists. As paintings they are primitive and awkward. Their forms are lumpy, their poses complicated, and each figure seems to have been studied on its own, to be joined to the others afterwards. Hands gesticulate, eyes are beady and mouths drawn down. The flesh even of quite young figures appears to be shrivelled up like a wizened apple. There is often a figure in the foreground in shadow seen from the back (Pl. 3). It is evident that, like many young artists, Rembrandt was keeping a close eye on the art around him and, knowing he would be judged by its standards, trying to outdo it. We can sense him hoping to win through by a display of skill. He would expect each figure to be admired in turn. At the same time, he was bolder than Lastman, who seems by comparison frightened of stepping outside the classical rules. He avoids Lastman's generalized forms and draperies; from the start Rembrandt is concerned with the particular. An individual vein of appealing sentiment informs the *Anna and Tobit* (Pl. 2), and there is an intriguing ambiguity about the figures in the *Two Scholars Disputing.* Who are they? Are they really scholars? named Greek philosophers? Old Testament prophets? These things strike a new, arresting note.

About 1630 Rembrandt steps back, as it were, from the subject and places the figures in the second plane in a high vaulted space. Perhaps attracted by indirect knowledge of Caravaggio, he makes the observation of a pool of light surrounded by darkness the visual motive of the picture. Where there is only one figure, this figure is often represented in contemplation or asleep, so that the shadowy atmospheric space above appears as an emanation of thought or dreams. Visually it is as if Rembrandt were standing at a distance watching the light as it fell from a high window in a dim Gothic interior. Similar but not identical means are used for the depiction in this setting of a lonely scholar seated by a window and the *Presentation of Jesus in the Temple* (Pl. 7). The difference is that, whereas in the secular scene the light has a visible source, in the latter the natural light is fused with a supernatural radiance emanating from the figure group; yet this is done so subtly that we are only subconsciously aware of it and the way the

light falls strikes us at first glance as natural. Rembrandt was to use this device again and again in religious pictures in the future.

The composition of the *Presentation* is absolutely calm. No one moves or speaks but everyone looks. It is a picture about looking, about understanding through the eyes. In the central group, gazes are fastened on Simeon holding the Christ-Child; he returns them in the direction of the high priest whose profile is lost in shadow. Other figures – grave Rabbis seated in the foreground, a more excited crowd dimly visible on the steps to the right – watch from a distance. Two old men from the crowd have come forward to join the central group, peering over Mary's shoulder. We recognize in them the many pen and ink studies of beggars which Rembrandt made from life during this period. Thus is reality blended with sacred history. The solemn mood leaves us in no doubt that we, like the onlookers in the painting, are witnesses to a divine revelation.

Within the scheme of light and shade, the composition is defined by lines: verticals in the figures and architecture, horizontals and receding diagonals along the steps and the divisions in the pavement. The vertical emphasis, which rises to a climax in the pillar to the right of centre, above the Infant Christ, rests on a firm base. The figures are also lineally conceived, but the lines fall as much within the forms, following the folds in drapery, as they do along their contours. We are again reminded of Rembrandt's drawings of this period, in which he used long looping strokes, hardly lifting his pen from the paper. The colours are cool and close to one another in the spectrum; the brushwork is delicate and the surface smooth and luminous like deeply polished wood, echoing the wooden panel on which it is painted.

The Presentation in the Temple, executed in 1631 about the time that Rembrandt left Leyden for Amsterdam, is one of his first masterpieces on a small scale. But, regarding his career as a whole, we must take account not only of the intimate, closed, spiritual Rembrandt; there is also the open, monumental, baroque Rembrandt to be remembered. Perhaps initially the decision to work on a large scale was the desire to emulate Rubens, who deeply affected Rembrandt's art in the early 1630s and was, after Lastman, the most important single influence in his career. Rubens's richly plastic modelling, though not his composition, is already reflected in the heads of *The Anatomy Lesson of Dr Tulp* (1632; Pls. 8, 9), with which Rembrandt made his reputation on his arrival in Amsterdam. Like most of Rembrandt's group portraits this is partly a subject picture, since it contains an action and figures responding to it. The painting represents a private dissection, which would have preceded or followed the public one held by the surgeons' guild. Dr Tulp is shown demonstrating the muscles and tendons of the forearm and comparing his findings with a diagram in a recently published book on anatomy, which has been identified. Nevertheless, the composition is as much that of a group portrait as of a documentary record, and the action, in addition to being basically true to life, is a device for unifying the picture. What contemporaries would have admired is Rembrandt's virtuosity as an artist: his invention, the vividness of the expressions, his smooth brushwork, and the skilful foreshortening of the naked corpse. In Amsterdam in 1632, this was what painting was about.

Belshazzar's Feast (Pl. 12), another large work of this decade which exhibits similar qualities, is still more ambitious. Whether it is equally successful is another question. Rembrandt, here unhampered by real life, gives his imagination free rein. It is a painting designed to impress. It displays difficult technical problems chosen and overcome: not only expression but lighting, movement and the treatment of exotic still-life accessories and costumes. Much is made of the play of both direct and reflected light on surfaces. This is especially true at the left, where the woman seated in the foreground seems literally bathed in iridescence. Softer, partly reflected light glances over the two figures facing Belshazzar, while another figure almost lost in shadow hovers dimly in the background. On the right a swaying, foreshortened figure reflects the influence of Venetian painting both in pose and in the painting of the red velvet sleeve. The composition is defined by powerful baroque diagonals anchored at the centre by the massive body of Belshazzar and focused on the great jewelled clasp of his cloak. The impasto is very thick and heavily worked in this area, as if mimicking the substance it is representing. The cloak, turban and trinkets would have been modelled on the bizarre costumes and curios with which Rembrandt stuffed his studio wardrobe.

This is perhaps Rembrandt's most purely theatrical painting. Everything in it is emphatic, exotic and astounding. Yet for most modern critics it is a failure. It seems to be too lacking in other qualities. The dramatic event which touches off the action – 'the Writing on the Wall' – is sensational enough to justify the rhetoric but we feel that Rembrandt is trying too hard. Wine spilling not just from one but from *two* goblets is too much. The expressions are overdone and the painting of Belshazzar's face and hands is ugly and grotesque. But it is at least – with some of the early self-portraits – a corrective to the sentimental view of Rembrandt. Only he could have carried off such a monstrous performance.

After this, Rembrandt progressively diminishes the area in which rich costumes and precious metals appear, yet until the last decade there is usually a hint of such richness somewhere in the picture, of brocades or burnished metals glowing like fire. Rhetoric also dies away and, from the early 1640s onwards, outflung arms and grimacing features – the outward, baroque means of conveying emotion – are replaced by subtle hints of feeling in the eyes, set of the head and pose.

The transition to a new kind of art was effected in a number of tranquil scenes painted during the 1640s, the common theme of which is domestic piety. We find this epitomized in the Old Testament (*Manoah and his Wife, Tobit and Anna*) as well as in the New (*The Holy Family*, Pl. 23, and *The Adoration of the Shepherds*). No mythological subjects were painted during this decade, even among the single figures. The most typical single figure is the impoverished, bearded old man, hatless or wearing a simple cap, seen head and shoulders only, and the young servant girl appearing at a window (Pl. 25). Whether this withdrawal into a more intimate kind of art was occasioned by reaction (Rembrandt's, not his contemporaries') against the bombast of the '*Night Watch*' (1642; Pls. 18, 19), by grief at the death of his wife, or by factors in his own interior life, is uncertain. Rembrandt's own thoughts and feelings, as distinct from their manifestations in his appearance (as seen in his self-portraits) lie outside our knowledge.

Perhaps the most significant development – it is even more important than the subject and composition – consists in the technique. A simple way of putting this is to say that the brushwork becomes broader, but there is more to it than that. The change affects the whole treatment of form. An alternative explanation might be to suggest that the top layers of paint have been left off and that the surface now visible is what would previously have been the underpainting or a sketch; in other words, one might describe the paintings, as the early critics described them, as unfinished. In fact they are not unfinished, nor did Rembrandt simply substitute sketches for finished pictures. On the whole he did not make preparatory sketches in oil except for some of his early etchings. Nevertheless, the analogy with the sketch and the first stages of a painting is one way of understanding the process by which the new technique was achieved. A glance at the monochrome sketch of the *Entombment of Christ* (Pl. 20) will illustrate this, as it shows what happens at its simplest and most extreme. Not only are the surfaces of the forms left out but the transitions between tones are omitted as well. A stroke of paint is used simultaneously to indicate the tone of a form and its approximate shape. Differing tones are placed side by side instead of being blended into one another. This brushwork is a kind of 'note form'. It is functional and without embellishments; it does not suggest movement or texture; it denotes rather than describes.

It could not be more different from the more highly finished parts of earlier paintings, like the *Presentation in the Temple*. There the brushwork follows the contours and internal modelling of the forms, describing their surface minutely. The tones are blended, the stroke is soft and linear. This even applies to more vigorously handled comparatively late works of the 1630s, like *The Risen Christ Appearing to the Magdalen* (Pl. 22). It is only in subsidiary parts of these paintings, which are not meant to attract the eye particularly and where the forms are slightly indistinct, that the simplified brushwork of the 'forties is anticipated. (Contrary to what might be expected, it does not seem to be anticipated in Rembrandt's most personal, and therefore most freely handled, early paintings, such as his portraits of himself and his family; the brushwork in these is looser but its descriptive character is the same as that of other works of the period.)

However, there are differences as well as similarities in Rembrandt's technique between his finished paintings of the 'forties and his sketches. For one thing, speed is of the essence in a sketch, and Rembrandt was not interested in speed; Baldinucci records that he was a slow worker, going over passages again and again, waiting for each layer to dry, until he was satisfied with the result. More important, the brushstrokes in the finished paintings of this period (e.g. *The Holy Family with Angels*, Pl. 23) are very refined and their shape is carefully calculated. Each one is unobtrusive yet of the utmost significance. It conveys simultaneously form, colour, texture and tone. To some extent the last three could be adjusted later by means of glazes but the form had to be exactly right from the first; its shape had to be defined exactly by the mark made by the brush. In some of the figures in smaller works, a complete head or hand may be represented by a single brushstroke, without modulations of tone. No more than three or four strokes are required for the headcloth of the Madonna in *The Holy Family with Angels*; another single broad stroke suffices for the piece of this cloth which comes over her right shoulder. In still later works (see the hands in the portrait of Jan Six, Pl. 36), proportionately fewer strokes are used for more complex forms. Nor are there many different tones in these forms. The main tonal variations are expressed by juxtaposition, not by blending. The slight changes which suggest the play of light and atmosphere over the forms are obtained by glazes. One advantage of this broader yet very precise method of handling was that Rembrandt could make larger, seemingly 'empty' areas visually interesting. He could avoid the fussiness which characterizes many of his paintings of the previous decade (Pl. 22). What earlier or contemporary painter could have made so commonplace an object as a child's wicker cradle seem so fascinating to the eye? The paint has a beauty in itself, over and above its representational function.

The brushwork also had another purpose: to represent emotion. Rembrandt was no longer interested in conveying expression by exaggerated facial movements, that is to say, by movements which he could describe by tracing their outlines with the brush. He knew that human emotions are often expressed by only very slight changes in the facial muscles – perhaps only around the eyes and at the corners of the mouth – changes which the observer in real life is able to pick up but which are too subtle to be represented by conventional formulas of expression. By placing the brushstroke just 'so', in the cheek below the eye or along the eyelid, Rembrandt was able to record these tiny movements and hence to imply the expression in the eye itself. This gave him, further, the power to convey a whole range of emotions that were outside the capacity of previous artists. This applies particularly to the inward or contemplative emotions of love, compassion and apprehension, as distinct from the outgoing and active ones of terror and rage. In his middle and later years Rembrandt hardly ever represented figures in violent states of feeling. Moreover, his mastery of expression was not confined to the treatment of faces; it is also evident in his painting of hands and indeed the whole body. No painter has made so much of the touching of one figure by another with a hand: the husband laying a hand on his wife's shoulder in *Jupiter and Mercury Visiting Philemon and Baucis* (Pl. 29); *Jacob Blessing the Children of Joseph* (Pl. 33); Mary reaching out a hand to lift the cloth from the Child's cradle without waking Him (Pl. 23).

The technical characteristics which have been discussed are epitomized in this last, the most beautiful and central painting of Rembrandt's middle years. To study it is to realize that what can be described as technique is not a dry mechanical dexterity but the counterpart of imaginative and spiritual qualities. Here is the familiar theme of the Madonna and Child represented in the costumes and setting of a *genre* scene (Goethe's 'Dutch peasant woman') but made sacred, not just by the presence of angels, but by the colour, expressions and brushwork. By keeping the colours and lighting very pure and by a slight emphasis on the regularity of certain forms – the line of Mary's shoulder, the oval of her face, the smoothness of her brow – Rembrandt invests the figure with a sweetness which proclaims that this is no ordinary mother but the Mother of God.

In Rembrandt's late art this sweetness is avoided. It is an art largely dominated by men: the Madonna hardly reappears; the characteristic female figure is *Lucretia* (Pl. 47). Many of the paintings are large. The figures are almost all life-size and are usually shown in three-quarter length. The conception of the pictures is monumental and austere, although it may encompass moods both of great tenderness ('*The Jewish Bride*', Pl. 39) and bitter humiliation (*The Disgrace of Haman* in Leningrad). The sentiment in the second of these paintings is conveyed entirely through facial expression and is not even fully apparent to a spectator ignorant of the story. Equally, the late pictures may include a strain of vivid realism, as in the *Two Negroes* (Pl. 46); or they may summon up ghosts. What apparitions are they, what survivors of some unknown Northern mythology, that gather round the table to swear the oath in *The Conspiracy of Julius Civilis* (Pl. 43)?

However, we are more conscious of what unites the late works than of what divides them. The trend is away from realism and narrative, and towards essence rather than existence. Even the expressions are often mute or inscrutable; the figures think and feel but no longer communicate as before. They embody a kind of super-real presence which is all the more intense for being without corresponding form or rational cause. The observation of light and shade is less illusionistic than before. The brushwork also almost ceases to have a representational function and to become, instead, an independent medium. We often cannot tell the material of which the costumes are made. The paint, applied in square overlapping patches, layer upon layer, scratched with the handle of the brush, scraped off and reapplied, has its own extraordinary character, its own vitality. The marks scarcely define the shape of forms; like the penstrokes in the late drawings or the drypoint lines in the late etchings, they lie outside or within, not along, the contours. Blocked in with straight edges, they serve as lines of force, indicating direction.

The forms, though massive in area, are insubstantial and flattened, and limbs that would normally be seen in foreshortening are sometimes distorted in order to bring them into a plane parallel with the picture surface. The integrity of the picture surface is all. What we see is a tapestry of colours and tones into which figures and faces are dimly yet palpably woven. A greater number of different tones and different shades of the same or related colours, each distinct yet harmonized with the others, is visible than in the work of any other artist, not even excepting the late Titian. The effect is at once dream-like and intensely vivid; subtle and overpoweringly impressive. Like the late work of some other great artists, Rembrandt's is essentially tragic. As the mind contemplates it, it is purged of the emotions of pity and terror and brought to a state of peace.

The Portraits

In discussing Rembrandt's portraits it is difficult not to begin with the cliché that he was the greatest portrait painter of all time. This statement does not take us very far; and if true, it imposes an obligation on the critic to explain why it should be so. At all events, it will generally be agreed that Rembrandt embodies most of our ideas of what a great portrait painter should be. Nowadays we think more highly of that type of portraiture which reveals character than of that which reveals mere likeness. We expect a portrait to uncover 'the real man', to show him warts and all and to disclose the private weaknesses behind the public face. We would rather that the painter were the critic than the flatterer of his sitters. Further, we ask that a portrait should tell us as much about the artist as about the person portrayed; that it should be the product of a collaboration between the two, the end in view being the creation of a work of art.

Now, these are democratic expectations, most of which previous ages did not share. It happens that Rembrandt – in a sense – satisfies them; the fact that he does so is one reason for his popularity today. But Rembrandt fulfils the modern requirements of portraiture to both a greater and lesser extent than might be expected. As usual, his method is not reducible to a formula; nor is it easy to group his portraits and single figures into categories for purposes of discussion. Although they all have some things in common, each turns out on examination to be a unique achievement.

The painting of a portrait poses two main artistic problems. The first, which applies to all representations of the single figure, is how to avoid monotony. It is one failing of the second-rate portrait painter that all his figures, apart from their features and sometimes clothing, tend to look alike. Even the very good portrait painter of the second rank, like Frans Hals, may, by emphasizing the pose and introducing gestures and movement, achieve only a superficial variety, since if these factors are overstressed they appear contrived. Rembrandt generally keeps the poses of his sitters quiet and unassuming, although they are never dull, and he rarely uses gesture or movement. Except in his earliest self-portraits the expressions are also restrained, and this becomes increasingly true in his later work; there is always something withheld from, as well as given to, the observer. Rembrandt's chief means of gaining variety are, one, the use of costumes and attitudes which show the sitter adopting a role (this is not confined to portraits of himself and his family, although it is most clearly evident there); and, two, the creation of a mood of introspection or internal drama, into which the observer finds himself drawn. This mood stimulates curiosity and produces a suggestion of 'content' which is like that of subject paintings, not just of portraits, and hence is capable of similar variations. By concentrating on the sitter's psychology, sometimes emphasizing one side of his personality by showing him acting a role, Rembrandt achieves a more genuine variety than he would have done if he had used more superficial means.

The second problem of portraiture is that of representing character. Ever since the Renaissance, it has been understood that the portrait painter has a duty to reveal the character of his sitters and not merely to copy their likeness. Until comparatively recently this did not mean probing the sitter's inner psychology; it was sufficient if his more salient virtues were displayed. The task presented no theoretical problem, since it was generally believed – following the basic premise of that popular intellectual game of the period, physiognomy – that 'the face is the index to the mind'. In practice, however, the achievement of this aim was very difficult, not so much because of the inherent limitations of the visual medium of painting, although these were serious enough, but because of a fallacy in the theory. Briefly, this fallacy was the assumption that it is possible to *deduce* a person's character by studying his features, whereas in fact his character can only be *recognized* by this means; in other words, the face only reveals character to those who know it already. To friends and contemporaries of the sitter, his portrait may reveal him 'to the life', but its doing so depends on their knowing him in life and being able to read into the portrait his typical expression, aspects of his character and so on, which are already familiar to them. To take a specialized case – one of the few recorded contemporary comments on Rembrandt as a portrait painter: the poet Vondel instructed Rembrandt, when portraying Jan Cornelisz. Anslo, who was a famous preacher in Amsterdam, 'to paint Cornelisz's voice'. Whether Vondel was satisfied with the result is not known, but Rembrandt's presumed success, even in the metaphorical sense in which Vondel meant it, is inevitably lost on us as we have no means of comparing the painting with the living model. It follows from this that a portrait can convey character to posterity to something like the extent it did to contemporaries only if the sitter is historically very well known; that is to say, if we possess written information about him which we can read into his portrait in the same way that contemporaries were able to apply their knowledge of him gained from life. Unfortunately none of Rembrandt's sitters is historically well known in this sense.

It does not seem that the significance of this aspect of the problem of portraying character found a place in Renaissance and seventeenth-century art theory. Nevertheless, painters appear to have grasped it intuitively from an early date and to have attempted to convey certain elements of a sitter's character by means which posterity could discern. One favourite method was to include symbolic attributes of the sitter's accomplishments or profession; another was the use of emblems; a third was idealization of the sitter's features and body, to emphasize his position in society and distinction of mind. Rembrandt, as might be expected, had a deeper understanding of the problem than any other painter, yet he used hardly any of the usual, mostly external, devices. His means were chiefly inward-looking and subjective – above all, the *chiaroscuro*. He used *chiaroscuro* to create an appropriate mood or a revealing play of emotions in the sitter's features. Alternatively, he would emphasize some features at the expense of others; thus in some of his self-portraits he adjusts the shadow down one side of his face to hide the bulbousness of his nose. In this type of self-portrait he presents himself as refined and relaxed, quietly confident of his powers; in other types the thickness of his features is unsparingly revealed and he appears aggressive when young or anguished when old. A further means of expressing character, as it is of achieving variety, is also common in Rembrandt's portraits. This is the casting of the figure in some guise or role by the use of costumes, the pose and, occasionally, associations of style. At one extreme this takes the form of dressing up or play acting, as in *Saskia as Flora* (Pl. 11). At the other extreme it may appear as a subtle emphasis on one side of a sitter's personality at the expense of others: slight adjustments to the composition and *chiaroscuro* in the portrait of Jacob Trip (Pl. 45) tend, without detracting from his individuality, to build him up into 'the man of authority'. In the same way, Rembrandt presents himself in his self-portraits now as 'the artist' (Pl. 48), now as 'the gentleman', and so on.

From all this it is evident that Rembrandt's depiction of character is far from being the total disclosure that it is sometimes made out to be (though it is significant that those who hold this view tend to be reticent as to the precise characteristics disclosed). What Rembrandt achieves is all that a painter can achieve, namely to show, by artistic means, certain qualities of a sitter's character that we might be able to recognize in his face if we knew him in life. It is in the nature of things that we cannot specify or label these qualities very exactly and that our understanding of them is subjective; yet, such is Rembrandt's skill, they can be identified within fairly narrow limits. Beyond these limits, Rembrandt gives us 'character' in a more general sense, as we say in the phrase 'this figure is full of character', or that person is 'a man of character'. He does this by making his figures look within themselves as well as out towards us, and by presenting them in a context of introspection and thought. These qualities will be discussed again in a moment but at this point it will be convenient to look at some examples of Rembrandt's portraiture in slightly more detail. They will be taken in approximate chronological order but the differences between them can be found at all stages of his career and only partly reflect a development in his approach.

The first is the enchanting *Saskia as Flora* in Leningrad of 1634 (Pl. 11). This is a costume piece like the well-known painting of the same subject in London, but the two are not identical in treatment. In the London *Saskia* we are very much aware of the contrast between the sitter and her costume, although this contrast is itself revealing and not merely awkward. It is a portrait of Saskia unaccustomed to this fancy dress. In the Leningrad painting the sitter, though still clearly recognizable as Saskia, has been more fully assimilated to the idea of a classical goddess. The

metamorphosis is not complete and is all the more touching for that, but Saskia's face is sweetened and she steps into her pastoral role with a grace that owes something to Titian and Rubens as well as to contemporary Dutch conventions of pastoral painting. Her pregnancy adds the idea of fertility to the traditional conception of the classical goddess of spring. The handling is smooth and the colours unusually clear and decorative for Rembrandt. Flowers appear in the background as well as in Saskia's hair and wound round her staff. The gesture of holding something lightly in the hand, as so often in Rembrandt, is an indication of informality; for example, Jan Six drawing on his gloves (Pl. 36) or Titus puzzling over his homework (Pl. 31). The picture sustains, fused and in perfect balance, a number of contrasting associations: those of reality, mythology and the stage. Is the figure Saskia dressed up as Flora, or an allegorical painting of Flora for which Saskia sat as a model? That the answer is in doubt is an index of the painting's position on the borderline between portraiture and mythology. It is at once a personal record of Rembrandt's affection for his wife – and hence it tells us something about one side of her personality – and a commentary on the pastoral convention of spring.

The treatment of the *Jacob Trip* (Pl. 45) is very different. Here, every stroke proclaims the idea of authority – the parallel verticals of the stick and the chair, the severely upright pose, the look in the heavy-lidded eyes, and the shadows which fall in such a way as apparently to lengthen the face. It happens that several other portraits of Trip by different artists are known, from which it can be seen that Rembrandt's is a good likeness. But the comparison also shows that it is very much more than a likeness. The versions by Cuyp and Maes tell us little more than that the sitter was an old man with a thin face and hooked nose. Rembrandt depicts the aged armaments manufacturer as a symbol of iron will-power. No Old Testament prophet or mythological sage in his *oeuvre* is as gaunt as this formidable ancient figure, who is both sinister and wise, a merchant patriarch of the new, Protestant Jerusalem which was Amsterdam. Even if the sitter's whole personality cannot be understood and if the presentation is one-sided, even though any interpretation is bound to be subjective – even though these things are true, there is no doubt that this is an image of 'character'. And it is achieved by aesthetic means: by the low viewpoint and imposing breadth of the lower part of the figure, by the massive cloak and archaic, throne-like chair, and, most subtly, by the *chiaroscuro*. This elongates the face and figure, widens the forehead and enlarges the eyes.

'*The Falconer*' (Pl. 41) is an equally impressive but more ambiguous work, at once tragic and flamboyant. Is it an imaginary historical portrait? a portrait of a character in a play? a painting of a model in invented clothes? Certainly it has a strange air of unreality: the horse, the groom, the bird – none of these look as if painted from life. Rembrandt seems here to bring back the baroque or Venetian fancy picture in a new guise. The powerful face is pictorially integrated with the rest of the composition yet appears psychologically detached from it. The large eyes are the focus of the picture yet register a blank stare. The brushwork, like the conception as a whole, is broad and vigorous and comparatively unbroken for the late date. The colour – hot red, orange and gold throughout – plays a more independent role than in earlier works and establishes the painting's mood. The model is one who appears frequently in Rembrandt's art around 1660 in a number of different guises – as Christ, as an apostle or as an unnamed bearded man. It is characteristic that his features and age should be varied in each of these representations. Rembrandt's ability to paint from the life and yet alter what he sees is often overlooked by those who try to interpret his portraits and studies of single figures too literally. This is particularly true of his use of his mistress, Hendrickje, as a model. The question, when confronted with a painting of a young or young-ish woman, 'is it Hendrickje?', often does not admit of a yes or no answer.

Contemplation or introspection is the *leitmotiv* of Rembrandt's mature and late portraits. Sunk in reverie or gazing towards the observer, the figures seem to exist in an atmosphere of their own. They are watchful yet withdrawn, and behind the eyes the mind is preoccupied by thought. Rembrandt began treating portraits and studies of old people in this way very early in his career, then applied the same method to his self-portraits, and finally extended it to all his portraits in varying degrees after 1640. As a conception of portraiture this was not without precedents: the *Mona Lisa* is one famous example and there are others of a slightly different kind in the work of Titian. But Rembrandt developed this type of portrait further than anyone else and used it for a far wider range of sitters. Although its most typical representatives are men accustomed to thought rather than action – doctors, preachers and artists – it is not confined to them.

Rembrandt's principal means is once more the *chiaroscuro*. The face normally receives the strongest light, which gives it the prominence which its importance in the portrait leads one to expect. At the same time the face is criss-crossed by shadows which both lend it interest and character and enmesh it, as it were, in the background. Shadows collect in and around the eyes and the hollows of the cheeks, down one side of the nose and round the mouth. Sometimes the eyes are heavily shaded by a hat. The edges where one tone meets another are softened, and it is frequently the side of the face turned towards the observer which is illuminated, thereby avoiding a sharply silhouetted cheek-line on the other side. The effect of all this is to divert attention from the face as a unit and transfer it to the features. The features, especially the eyes, thus become all the more telling as indicators of mood and character. Yet for all their rich expressiveness they remain partly inscrutable, for two reasons. The first reason is that the eyes are defined by the shadows, not by the light, which gives them a far-away look, as if there were some invisible force uniting them with the background (it is remarkable how much more aggressive – and less interesting – the faces in Rembrandt's portraits appear if they are looked at with the backgrounds masked off). The second reason is that the expressions are not superficially animated. Rembrandt's sitters may watch the observer intently; they do not communicate with him. Their eyes are steady and their

mouths closed. Animation lies in the technique – the fluid *impasto*, the delicate and varied glazing, the play of atmosphere and light and shade over the features; it does not lie in the features themselves.

This is a conception of portraiture that belongs at the opposite pole from arrested movement; the impression is rather one of immobility and timelessness. It follows that Rembrandt's portraits stand not just for the likeness and characterization of individuals. Nor do they add up to 'the portrait of an epoch'; they are not social documents. While each portrait is unique and each records the lineaments of a particular person, it carries overtones which make the individual the representative of suffering humanity. At bottom what Rembrandt portrays is the human predicament. And he saw that predicament as both tragic and watched over by a mysterious spiritual force. It is not for nothing that critics have seen a resemblance between Rembrandt's paintings and the philosophical ideas of his fellow resident of Amsterdam, Spinoza (although the latter was too young to have influenced him). Both men were steeped in the Jewish scriptures, and Rembrandt would have shared Spinoza's doctrine of the integration of spirit and matter. The mystery which permeates Rembrandt's shadows is ultimately a metaphor of the immanence of God.

There is one further characteristic of Rembrandt's portraiture: the intensity of the relationship between the sitter and the observer. Although in one sense Rembrandt's sitters are remote from us, in another sense they are vividly real. They are vulnerable to scrutiny and, wearing no social mask, they draw us into their world. The experience of looking at them is essentially private; it excludes the presence of a third person and exposes the observer to his own thoughts and feelings as much as it reveals those of the person portrayed (contrast Frans Hals, whose sitters often seem to be looking over the observer's shoulder at someone else). There is some reason to believe that Rembrandt always wanted his paintings to be contemplated very intimately. He interposed first the background, then the frame, as a barrier between the painted image and the outside world – this was the reverse of the baroque principle of extending the created world of the painting into the observer's space. In two cases, not portraits (one is Pl. 38), Rembrandt indicated the type of frame he would like: it was a kind of tabernacle, with pilasters either side, a 'base' and a curved or pedimented top. In a third example, *The Holy Family with a Cat* (Pl. 28), such a frame, together with a curtain half drawn in front of the scene, actually forms part of the picture.

To be exact, the contemplation of Rembrandt's portraits usually involves three people: the sitter, the observer and the artist. But there was one category in which this number was reduced to two: the self-portraits. Perhaps it is not altogether fanciful to see this factor as an additional, aesthetic reason, over and above the personal and autobiographical ones, for the quantity of self-portraits in Rembrandt's *oeuvre*. In the self-portrait he was able to address the observer directly, without the distraction of another personality. If a portrait becomes a work of art as the result of a collaboration between the sitter and the artist, the collaboration is made easier when sitter and artist are one. When painting himself Rembrandt was freer to vary his interpretation by adopting a wider range of poses, costumes and lighting effects than he could use in his commissioned portraits; he could treat himself as either sitter or model, that is, he could depict himself either more or less realistically; and, knowing himself better than he knew anyone else, he could make the self-portrait a more effective vehicle of character. He was sufficiently self-absorbed to represent his own features at least twice a year throughout his working life; and he did so for the most part not in the casual or experimental media of drawings and oil sketches but in finished paintings and, to a lesser extent, etchings. Many of these painted self-portraits are as highly wrought as any portraits in his *oeuvre*. It is not impossible that there was a market for them (significantly, not one is listed in the inventory of his possessions drawn up in 1656, although many of his other paintings and oil sketches appear there). If Rembrandt's self-portraits constitute a diary, as in a sense they do, it was a diary at least partly intended for publication.

Nevertheless, his self-absorption was accompanied by a remarkable objectivity. In his youth he was bold enough not to disguise his conceit; in his maturity and old age he became his own severest critic. To call Rembrandt's self-portraits his greatest achievement would be to fall into the trap of sentimentalizing him. It would also be incorrect. But they are in some ways the purest expression of his approach to portraiture.

A Note on the Landscapes

As we have seen, Rembrandt was not a *genre* painter, although he made many drawings of *genre* scenes from life. It would be impossible to deny that he was a landscape painter, but the same distinction applies; that is, he made numerous landscape drawings from nature but very few landscape paintings of a similar character. Apart from these exceptions, all his landscape paintings were imaginary, and they were all executed, including the few naturalistic ones (Pl. 24b), during his middle period, between about 1636 and 1655. As with his treatment of *genre*, the gap between drawings and paintings was bridged by the etchings, which are partly naturalistic and partly verging on the imaginary.

Objectively it is hard to understand the gulf between the two categories. As a landscape draughtsman from nature, Rembrandt was one of the most brilliant and inventive of all artists; light and air vibrate between every stroke of his rapid sketches of the open Dutch countryside. Rembrandt's paintings, on the other hand, are motionless and claustrophobic, despite their romantic intensity (Pl. 13). To a greater extent than any of Rembrandt's other works they fall into a category of their own in the history of art. Whereas his subject pictures, painted figure studies and portraits entered the mainstream of later European painting, his landscape paintings have had only an occasional influence (for example, on English watercolours around 1800). Rembrandt's landscapes seem to deny one of the basic principles of the art: interest in the mutually supporting roles of space, light and air. Instead, these elements tend to contradict one another in his work. While the arbitrary relationship between the light and shade pattern and the composition is an effective source of visual surprise, it prevents the landscape from expanding outwards to the sides or backwards into depth as far as the horizon. The exceptions to this tendency prove the rule, for they occur not in his imaginary landscapes proper but in the background of a figure painting – the '*Noli me tangere*' (Pl. 24a) – or in the naturalistic *Winter Landscape* (Pl. 24b). These at least are beautifully fresh.

Yet Rembrandt's landscape paintings may become more intelligible if they are seen in the context of his own aesthetic attitudes. Like his ideas of architecture and costume, he evolved his conception of landscape independently of the classical tradition, that is, independently of the conventions of ideal landscape painting. Rembrandt's antiquity is an imaginary Hebraic antiquity (derived if anything from Turkish sources), developed as an alternative to the Greek and Roman antiquity of Italian and Italianizing artists. Almost the only thing his landscapes have in common with ideal landscapes is that they are not naturalistic. But unlike ideal landscapes, and unlike the landscapes of that other great Northern inventor of imaginary scenes – Rubens – Rembrandt's landscape paintings have no real basis in the study of nature. Nor, unlike his drawings, are they Dutch in topography, although they show some Dutch stylistic influences. As was the case with his treatment of *genre* scenes, he transposed the subject matter of his landscapes – nature – on to the plane of religious art. They have that brooding, numinous quality which informs so much of his work. They conform once more, if only negatively, that the true subject of Rembrandt's art is man.

Outline Biography

1606 Rembrandt Harmensz van Rijn born on 15 July at Leyden, the son of Harmen Gerritsz. van Rijn, miller, and Neeltgen Willemsdochter van Zuidbroeck, daughter of a baker. He was the last but one in a family of seven.

1620 20 May: Rembrandt entered at Leyden University. His stay there, which was short, was presumably preceded by about 7 years spent in the Latin School at Leyden.

1620–4 Period of apprenticeship: three years with Jacob Isaaksz. van Swanenburgh in Leyden; six months with Pieter Lastman in Amsterdam; perhaps also a short time with Jacob Pynas.

1625 Rembrandt returns to Leyden and sets up as an independent painter, sharing a studio with Jan Lievens (1607–74), a former pupil of Lastman.

1628 February: Gerard Dou (1613–75) becomes Rembrandt's first pupil, remaining with him perhaps until 1631/2.

1630 Death of Rembrandt's father.

1631/2 Between 8 March 1631 and 26 July 1632, Rembrandt settles permanently in Amsterdam, lodging first with the dealer, Hendrik van Uylenburgh, in the Breestraat.

1633 5 June: betrothal to Saskia van Uylenburgh (1612–42), the daughter of a former burgomaster of Leeuwarden and a cousin of Hendrik van Uylenburgh.

1634 22 June: marriage to Saskia at Sint-Annaparochie, near Leeuwarden.

1635 15 December: baptism of Rembrandt's and Saskia's first child, Rumbartus (buried 15 February 1636).

1638 22 July: baptism of second child, Cornelia, called Cornelia I (buried 13 August 1638).

1639 12 January: Rembrandt is living in the Sugar Refinery on the Binnen Amstel. On 1 May he moves into a grand house, for which he is unable to pay, in the Breestraat.

1640 29 July: baptism of third child, called Cornelia II (buried 12 August 1640). On 14 September, Rembrandt's mother is buried in St Peter's Church, Leyden.

1641 22 September: baptism of fourth and only surviving child of Rembrandt and Saskia – Titus.

1642 14 June: death of Saskia.

1649 1 October: first reference to Hendrickje Stoffels (c. 1625–63) as living in Rembrandt's household.

1654 30 October: baptism of Hendrickje's child, Cornelia.

1656 17 May: Rembrandt transfers the legal ownership of his house to Titus. 25 and 26 July: inventory of the contents of the house in the Breestraat drawn up by the Court of Insolvency. His appeal for the liquidation of his property, to avoid being declared a bankrupt, had been agreed shortly before.

1657 December: first sale of Rembrandt's possessions.

1658 1 February: the house in the Breestraat auctioned for 11,218 guilders (nearly 2,000 guilders less than Rembrandt had paid in 1639), although for legal reasons Rembrandt probably continued to live there until 1660. 14 February: further sale of possessions authorized. 24 September: final sale authorized of remaining prints and drawings in Rembrandt's collection, including many of his own (total, 600 guilders).

1660 Rembrandt moves to a smaller house in the Rozengracht. Titus and Hendrickje form a company for dealing in works of art, with Rembrandt as their employee.

1663 24 July: burial of Hendrickje Stoffels in the Westerkerk.

1668 10 February: marriage of Titus to Magdalena van Loo. On 7 September Titus is buried in the Westerkerk. A daughter, Titia, is born to Magdalena and baptized on 22 March 1669.

1669 4 October: Rembrandt dies in the house in the Rozengracht. He is buried in the Westerkerk, Amsterdam, on 8 October.

List of Plates

1. *Self-Portrait*. About 1629–30. Amsterdam, Rijksmuseum

2. *Anna Accused by Tobit of Stealing the Kid*. 1626. Amsterdam, Rijksmuseum (on loan from Baroness Bentinck-Thyssen)

3. *Two Scholars Disputing*. 1628. Melbourne, National Gallery of Victoria

4. *Rembrandt's Mother* (?). About 1629–30. Windsor Castle (reproduced by Gracious Permission of Her Majesty the Queen)

5. *An Officer*. About 1629–30. Private Collection

6. *An Artist in his Studio*. About 1628–9. Boston, Museum of Fine Arts

7. *The Presentation of Jesus in the Temple.* 1631. The Hague, Mauritshuis

8. *Doctor Nicolaes Tulp Demonstrating the Anatomy of the Arm.* 1632. The Hague, Mauritshuis

9. Detail of Plate 8

10. *A Young Woman in Fancy Dress*. 163(5?). Château de Pregny, Geneva, Baron Edmond De Rothschild

11. *Saskia as Flora*. 1634. Leningrad, Hermitage

12. *The Feast of Belshazzar: The Writing on the Wall.* About 1635. London, National Gallery

13. *Landscape with a Church*. About 1640–5. Madrid, Duke of Berwick and Alba

14. *Self-portrait*. About 1639. Los Angeles, Norton Simon Collection

15. *Uzziah Stricken with Leprosy* (?). 1635. Chatsworth, Derbyshire, The Trustees of the Chatsworth Settlement

16. *Portrait of Agatha Bas.* 1641. London, Buckingham Palace (reproduced by Gracious Permission of Her Majesty the Queen)

17. *Portrait of the Painter Hendrick Martensz. Sorgh.* 1647. London, The Trustees of the 2nd Duke of Westminster and Anne, Duchess of Westminster

18. *The Militia Company of Captain Frans Banning Cocq ('The Night Watch')*. 1642. Amsterdam, Rijksmuseum

19. Detail of Plate 18

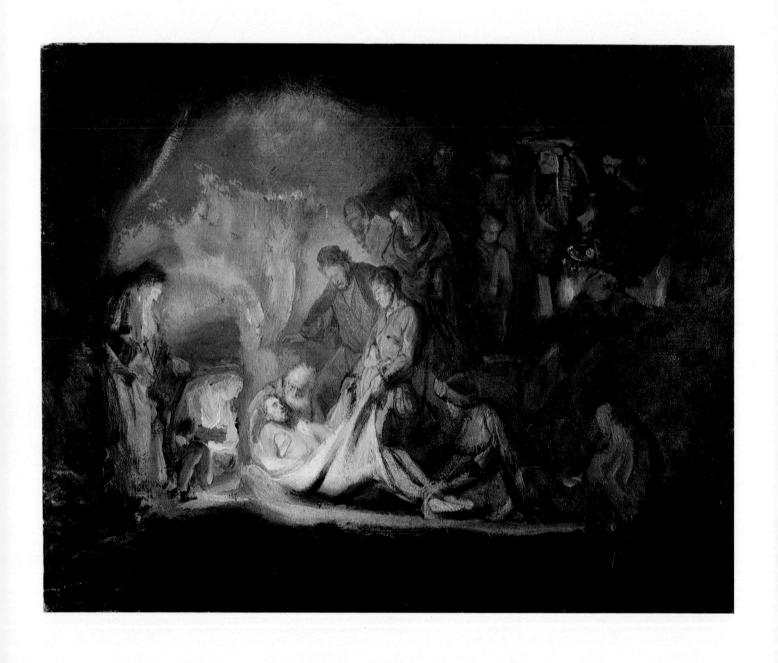

20. *The Entombment of Christ*. About 1636–8 (?). Glasgow University, Hunterian Museum

21. *Christ and the Woman Taken in Adultery*. 1644. London, National Gallery

22. *The Risen Christ Appearing to the Magdalen* ('*Noli Me Tangere*'). 1638. London, Buckingham Palace (reproduced by Gracious Permission of Her Majesty the Queen)

23. *The Holy Family with Angels*. 1645. Leningrad, Hermitage

24a. Detail of the landscape from *The Risen Christ Appearing to the Magdalen* (Plate 22)

24b. *Winter Landscape.* 1646. Cassel, Gemäldegalerie

25. *A Young Girl Leaning on a Window Sill.* 1645. London, Dulwich College Gallery

26. *A Woman Bathing* (Hendrickje Stoffels?). 1654. London, National Gallery

27. *Head of Christ*. About 1650 (?). Berlin-Dahlem, Gemäldegalerie

28. *The Holy Family with a Cat* (with painted frame and curtain). 1646. Cassel, Gemäldegalerie

29. *Jupiter and Mercury Visiting Philemon and Baucis*. 1658. Washington, D.C., National Gallery of Art (Widener Collection)

30. *Hendrickje Stoffels in a Fur Wrap*. About 1654. London, National Gallery

31. *Portrait of Titus*. 1655. Rotterdam, Boymans-van Beuningen Museum

32. 'The Polish Rider'. About 1655. New York, The Frick Collection

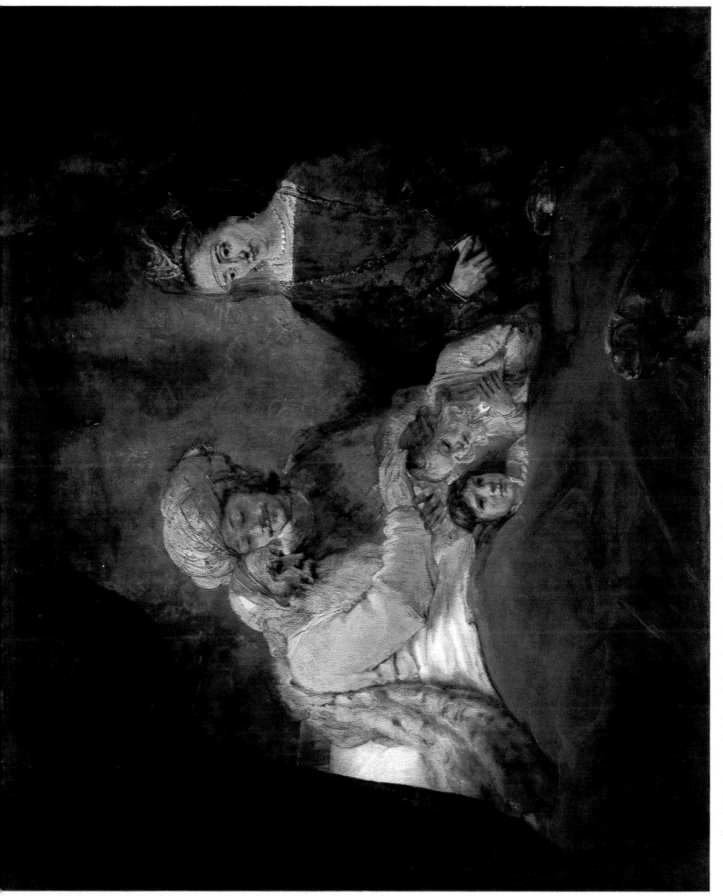

33. *Jacob Blessing the Children of Joseph.* 1656. Cassel, Gemäldegalerie

34. Detail of Plate 33

35. Detail of Plate 33

36. *Portrait of Jan Six*. 1654. Amsterdam, The Six Foundation

37. *An Old Woman Reading.* 1655. Drumlanrig Castle, Scotland, Duke of Buccleuch

38. *The Anatomy Lesson of Doctor Joan Deyman* (fragment). 1656. Amsterdam, Rijksmuseum

39. 'The Jewish Bride'. 1666(?). Amsterdam, Rijksmuseum

40. *The Apostle Bartholomew*. 1661. Malibu, John Paul Getty Collection

41. '*The Falconer*'. About 1661. Gothenburg, Museum

42. *The Sampling-Officials of the Cloth-Makers' Guild at Amsterdam* ('The Syndics'). 1662. Amsterdam, Rijksmuseum

43. *The Conspiracy of Julius Civilis: The Oath*. 1661–2. Stockholm, Nationalmuseum

44. *Portrait of a Woman Holding an Ostrich-Feather Fan*. About 1665–8. Washington, D.C., National Gallery of Art (Widener Collection)

45. *Portrait of Jacob Trip*. About 1661. London, National Gallery

46. *Two Negroes*. 1661. The Hague, Mauritshuis

47. *The Suicide of Lucretia*. 1666. Minneapolis, Institute of Arts

48. *Self-Portrait* (detail). About 1660. London, Kenwood House, The Iveagh Bequest